THE ULTIMATE MORTGAGE GUIDE

THE ULTIMATE MORTGAGE GUIDE
How to Secure the Best Mortgage Not Just the Best Rate

Copyright © 2023 Dante Royster

ISBN (paperback): 978-1-956220-60-5
ISBN (hardcover): 978-1-956220-63-6

Expert Press

www.ExpertPress.net

Expert Press
2 Shepard Hills Court
Little Rock, AR 72223
www.ExpertPress.net

Editing by Sharon Buck
Copyediting by Hannah Skaggs
Proofreading by Abby Kendall
Text design and composition by Emily Fritz
Cover design by Casey Fritz

The Ultimate Mortgage Guide

How to Secure the Best Mortgage
Not Just the Best Rate

Dante M. Royster
Founder of Epic Mortgage

CONTENTS

INTRODUCTION

"CAN YOU HELP US?" the middle-aged couple sitting in front of me asked nervously. They were holding hands. I was young, recently licensed as a mortgage broker, and they were my very first clients.

They owned a home in Chicago and were distressed about their financial situation, very concerned their home would be foreclosed on. They were also unsophisticated when it came to mortgages and refinancing their property.

After hearing their story, I was nervous because this was my first time, but I told them I would walk them through the fire and refinance their home. I held their hands each step of the way.

In the end, I got it done, they paid off some of their outstanding debt, and I saved them over a thousand dollars on their total monthly debt obligations. I felt so good that I was able to help them. I was, and still am, driven to support more people in getting a mortgage and changing their lives for the better.

You may wonder whether it's possible for you to attain the American Dream of owning your own home. Or maybe you're curious about whether there are ways to reduce your current mortgage payment or restructure your debt obligations. Clients ask me numerous questions about mortgages every day to see if one of those solutions could fit their needs. It all boils down to one very simple question: can I assist you in finding the right mortgage? The short answer is yes.

Mortgages, and all the financial jargon that comes with them, can be overwhelming. It's not that you're stupid, just that you may never have been taught this in school or you may not know the right questions to ask.

Not to worry. *The Ultimate Mortgage Guide* walks you through the basics of mortgages, the hows and the whys—without boring you. You'll see real-life examples of how learning about mortgages helped people obtain a new lease on life. You may even recognize yourself and your situation in one of the chapters.

I'm licensed as a mortgage broker in nine different states. This allows me to meet a lot of people from different walks of life and with various personal and financial situations. During the process, I'm also going to be your mortgage coach. Since I'm your coach, it's only fair that you ask what qualifies me to guide you through the sometimes-complicated maze of mortgages. You may also want to know a little bit about my background.

I was raised in a two-parent household until I was twelve, and then my parents divorced. This is not a typical divorce story in which everything was acrimonious, and I never saw one of my parents again. My parents were very involved in my upbringing.

As a child, I was into sports and music. My dad had the gift of gab, was my sports coach outside of school, and was my role model growing up. My mother was a loving and caring mom who allowed me freedom if I earned it. My mom was a teacher. She is the best mom.

I had great parents, and what they taught me has enabled me tremendously in the mortgage industry. I started in the mortgage business in June 2002, working for a direct lender. During the real estate collapse starting in 2007, I wanted to stay in the mortgage business, but I needed additional income to pay my bills, so I ended up founding my first business: Full Court Services, a sales company. I was moonlighting to help pay the bills so I could continue to grow my clientele. I started with nothing—no fancy offices, no huge debt, just my grit and determination. I hustled like crazy so I could build my mortgage business enough to open up my second business, Epic Mortgage, a regional mortgage brokerage firm.

Being a mortgage broker provides me with the opportunity to educate the consumer as well as to talk with various people every day. I love the competitive nature of the industry. I love finding new clients and building a long-term relationship with them. I am not a one-and-done type of broker.

I help people achieve the American Dream. I see the value of owning a home from an emotional standpoint as well as an economic one. My home allowed me to achieve some of my personal goals.

Mortgages aren't just about numbers; they're about helping people create a life. They build emotional security for your future. Let me help you understand mortgages and make your American Dream real.

1
WHAT IS A MORTGAGE?

WE NEED TO GO OVER SOME basic definitions of common terms in the mortgage industry so you can understand the most important concepts related to obtaining a mortgage.

The basic definition of a mortgage is a legal agreement in which a bank or other creditor lends money and charges interest in exchange for the title of the debtor's property. It's really just a fancy name for a loan. Once the loan is paid off, ownership of the title, sometimes called conveyance, belongs to the debtor—the person who paid the loan. Typically, mortgages are offered by banks or other financial institutions and involve borrowing money to pay for the property. That money is repaid over a period of time along with interest.

The property is used as collateral for the loan. That means if the borrower is unable to repay the loan, the lender has the right to take possession of the property through foreclosure.

Mortgages usually require a down payment. Typically, the down payment can range from 3 to 35 percent of the property's purchase price. The interest rate for the mortgage can also vary depending on the borrower's credit score, the size of the down payment, and the loan program you choose.

What does the above really mean to you? Say you've found the house or condo you want to purchase. You don't have the money to buy the home outright, so you borrow the money from a lending institution, such as a bank, to purchase it and you pay the lender back with interest on the amount they loaned you over a period of time.

HOW TO UTILIZE YOUR MORTGAGE

Residential mortgages aren't just for homes. You can buy condos, townhomes, multi-units, or apartment buildings. There are four basic reasons mortgages are used: property purchase, property renovations, debt restructuring, and cash-out refinancing for needs and wants. Let me explain the basic idea behind refinancing, and then we'll look closer at each of these reasons for taking out a mortgage.

A refinance is very similar to the initial mortgage process. Lenders will assess your creditworthiness, income, debt-to-income ratio, and the current value of your home. It also involves closing costs, which similarly include lender fees, appraisal fees, title search and insurance, and other fees. It's important to factor in these costs when evaluating the potential savings or benefits of refinancing.

A refinance can be used for various purposes. One common reason to refinance is to take advantage of lower interest rates. If market interest rates have dropped since you obtained your original mortgage, refinancing can allow you to secure a new loan with a lower rate. This can result in lower monthly mortgage payments. Some other common uses are home improvements, debt consolidation, education expenses, medical bills, or other financial needs.

Refinancing also provides an opportunity to change the length of your loan term. For example, you may choose to refinance from a thirty-year mortgage to a fifteen-year mortgage so you can pay off your loan faster. This will increase your monthly payments, but it can save you thousands of dollars in interest costs.

Now let's consider reasons you might take out a mortgage.

PROPERTY PURCHASE

Susie and John are in their mid-thirties. They've been together for several years, and they're eager to take the next step in their relationship: to purchase their first home together. Both have always rented and lived in apartments. They've been looking at various properties and think they have finally found something they can afford. They don't have the full purchase price on hand, so a mortgage will enable them to purchase their first home.

PROPERTY RENOVATIONS

Whether you're buying or refinancing a home, renovation is an opportunity to upgrade the existing decor or structure. Some buyers have an interest in fixing up a property to sell it for a higher price. Others see an eyesore, and the potential comes into view only after some tender loving care. Depending on the location, you may see an opportunity to buy the ugly duckling you hope to live in at a lower price, and then look to spruce it up. Others who have been living in a house may see opportunity in doing some upgrades in their house.

Marti owns an older home and had what she thought was a small electrical problem. Turned out the wiring in her home was not up to the current code, and she had to replace all of it. In this particular case, her house was paid for, and she could obtain a mortgage to make the needed repairs.

In another case, Reuben had been paying on his mortgage for approximately ten years when he had a major roof leak. He had made his payments on time and had a decent credit score. He obtained a second mortgage on his home so he could have a new roof put on.

DEBT RESTRUCTURING

Debbie and Tommy never had enough money. They ate out or ordered food three to five times a week. They went on very nice vacations two or three times a year. They bought new cars every two years. Each of them made a nice income, so, theoretically, they could afford their life-style. The bad news was they charged everything to their credit cards and made the minimum payments. There was no way they were ever going to get out of debt by doing that. On the brink of divorce due to their financial situation, they finally went to a marriage counselor, who referred them to a financial advisor.

They secured a second mortgage on their home, paid off their credit card balances, and now have only one card between them for emergency use only. They curtailed their spending and are jointly working on paying off their second mortgage.

A cautionary comment here: if you restructure your debt by taking out a second mortgage but don't change your spending habits, you will find yourself in much greater debt with virtually no way out.

CASH-OUT REFINANCING

A cash-out refinance is a way to take advantage of your home's value. If you have equity in your home, meaning the home's value is greater than what you owe on it, you can take out a new loan that gives you cash based on the difference between those amounts.

Dan had a daughter who wanted to go to college. As we all know, tuition is expensive. Dan cashed out his mortgage and used the funds to pay for his daughter's college education.

Cory was an older gentleman who wanted to celebrate his fiftieth anniversary with his wife in style. He did a cash-out to borrow $20,000 for a cruise.

TYPES OF MORTGAGES

Three common types of mortgages are fixed-rate, adjustable, and reverse mortgages. It's imperative that you know the difference between them and the advantages of each one.

FIXED-RATE MORTGAGE

Fixed-rate mortgages are the most common for residential homeowners and come with the following advantages:

- CONSISTENT MONTHLY PAYMENTS. The interest rate and monthly payment stay the same for the entire term of the loan. This makes it easier for the borrower to plan their budget.

- A CONSISTENT INTEREST RATE. You'll have peace of mind knowing the interest rate is going to stay the same even if the current interest rate soars past what you are currently paying.

· A SIMPLE STRUCTURE. They are easier to understand and make it easier for the borrower to compare rates from different lending institutions.

Lakesha and Tyrone are a young married couple with two toddlers. They saved money for a down payment and found a house they could afford. They wanted a mortgage that was affordable, with a payment that would stay the same throughout the length of the mortgage and would let them plan their budget around it.

On the other hand, these are some of the disadvantages of a fixed-rate mortgage:

· A HIGHER INITIAL INTEREST RATE. This common feature means the borrower may end up paying more over the life of the loan.

· PENALTIES FOR PAYING EARLY. There may be a penalty for prepayment of the loan or for making additional payments to the principal of the loan.

In Lakesha and Tyrone's mortgage, they are allowed to make additional payments to the principal of the loan without a penalty. Be sure to ask your mortgage broker about prepayment penalties.

ADJUSTABLE-RATE MORTGAGE (ARM)

With an adjustable-rate mortgage, your home loan's interest rate may change on a periodic basis. An ARM typically has a lower initial interest rate for a specified period of time and then adjusts to a predetermined economic index.

You may have heard of a 5/1 ARM. In this type of loan, the interest rate is fixed or stable for the first five years, and then it adjusts annually. The interest rate can either increase or decrease depending on the current market conditions. Your monthly mortgage payment may also increase or decrease according to the market interest rates.

Brianna and Jerome wanted to get in on purchasing a home before the prices zoomed any higher. They weren't concerned about the interest rate being flexible because they only wanted to get into a home and then flip it within a couple of years.

The following are some advantages of an ARM:

- LOWER MONTHLY PAYMENT. This feature means they can be beneficial to borrowers who want to sell or refinance their homes within a short amount of time. Also, if the interest rates decrease, your monthly payment can also decrease, which means you may save money over the loan's life.

· PAYMENT ADJUSTABILITY. You may have adjustability of your payments where, if your income is irregular, you may be able to pay interest only on your home loan.

· EASIER QUALIFICATION. It may be easier to qualify for an ARM than a fixed-rate mortgage.

But keep in mind that there are also some real disadvantages of an ARM:

· INTEREST RATE CHANGES CAN LEAD TO HIGHER PAYMENTS. You may discover there is a substantial payment increase after the initial fixed-rate period ends.

· UNCERTAINTY. You don't know what your monthly mortgage payment is going to be in the future. If you decide to refinance the ARM, you may be subject to additional closing costs and fees.

- Penalties for refinancing / early payment. If you decide to refinance to a fixed-rate mortgage, some ARMs have a prepayment penalty, which can mean a substantial loss of savings on the interest paid into the loan. Check to see if there are penalties for paying off your loan early.

- Negative amortization. Serious heads-up on this—some ARMs may allow for negative amortization, which means your monthly loan payment is less than the interest due, and this can increase your loan balance. It also means you may owe more on the loan than the property is worth.

You need a professional mortgage broker to help you carefully consider the pros and cons of an ARM prior to obtaining one.

Reverse Mortgage

Mary Edith was a widow and seventy-four years old. She was concerned that her monthly Social Security income (SSI) wasn't going to be enough for her to live on for the rest of her life. She consulted a financial advisor, who advised her to investigate a reverse mortgage. In her particular situation, she qualified for it.

Reverse mortgages are only for homeowners who are sixty-two years old or older. This allows them to convert a portion of their home equity into cash without having to sell their home or make monthly mortgage payments.

The homeowner can choose to receive the funds from the lender as a lump sum, a line of credit, or monthly payments. The amount can vary and depends on the homeowner's age, the value of the home, and the current interest rate.

A reverse mortgage does not have to be repaid until the homeowner moves out or passes away. When this happens, the home is sold, and the proceeds are used to repay the loan. If there is any remaining equity in the home, it is distributed to the homeowner's heirs.

In my opinion, a financial advisor or loved ones should discuss this option with the homeowner before they agree to move forward with a reverse mortgage.

Are you totally confused and bewildered about mortgages now? Let me make your life easier. You can always stop at any time in this book and give me a call at (708) 905-5300 or send me an email at:

DANTE@EPIC.MORTGAGE.

2
WHO YOU WORK
WITH MATTERS

HERE'S WHY MORTGAGE BROKERS ARE ESSENTIAL.

Steve and Dorothy knew a little bit about mortgages. They understood the basic differences between fixed-rate and adjustable-rate mortgages. Steve's best friend was telling him he could get a mortgage at his own credit union and didn't need a mortgage broker because "they cost you more money."

Dorothy was referred to me by a previous client who had a great experience. She wasn't sure whether Steve should go to the credit union, or they should just use me, the mortgage broker. She thought that there were so many variables in their current situation and that the purchase of a home was such a major decision. She was receiving a lot of input from family members, coworkers, and friends who all had different experiences, and she didn't want to end up choosing the wrong mortgage. Since her friend recommended her to me, and after much discussion with Steve, they agreed to meet with me for a second opinion.

Prospective home buyers are often tempted to DIY the process of getting a home loan because they're uninformed about the difference a mortgage broker can make. Let me tell you what a mortgage broker will do for you.

WHAT DO MORTGAGE BROKERS DO?

In our initial consultation, Steve was adamant that mortgage brokers were going to add thousands more to the cost of his and Dorothy's mortgage. He was sure he could do everything with his own credit union and save money.

I explained to him that mortgage brokers are paid in several different ways. It depends on the lender and the type of loan. Steve, like many others, was unaware that there are two basic ways mortgage brokers are paid.

First is the lender-paid commission, when the lender pays the mortgage broker a commission for arranging the loan. Typically, it's a percentage of the loan amount and is paid by the lender once the loan is funded.

The one Steve was most concerned about was the borrower-paid commission. This is when the borrowers, Steve and Dorothy, pay the broker directly for their services. The feature could be a flat fee or a percentage of the loan amount and is typically paid at closing. I assured Steve that a broker is not compensated for their time and expertise in just one way. I encouraged him to ask questions.

It's important for borrowers to ask questions, specifically including how their mortgage broker is being paid. Ask your mortgage broker for specifics on the fees or commissions. When there's anything you don't understand, ask questions.

MORTGAGE BROKERS ARE YOUR NEW BEST FRIEND

We have specialized knowledge in the mortgage industry and in your local area, especially about lenders and the type of mortgage you need. We know which lenders have the best interest rates and, more importantly, which ones are best for your budget and financial situation.

Finding the right lender at the right interest rate is very time-consuming and involves research, paperwork, and negotiation with the lender. It's not for the faint of heart. Today's mortgages are extremely competitive with lots of moving parts.

Trying to eliminate a broker can cost you a lot of money. You may not know about or understand loan terms, interest rate fluctuations, fees, or the differences between lending institutions. Without knowing the right questions to ask, you're setting yourself up for a failure that could cost you thousands.

Mortgage brokers have established working relationships with many lending institutions and can find the ones that will provide the best mortgage for your needs.

How Mortgage Brokers Help You Find the Right Mortgage

We've already discussed various types of mortgages. But other mortgage products may be available to you, and here are some to consider.

A "non-QM," or non-qualifying mortgage, is a type of mortgage loan that does not meet the standards or qualifications set by the Consumer Financial Protection Bureau. Non-QM loans may have riskier provisions, such as interest-only payments or additional income documentation requirements. They may be a good option for borrowers who can't meet the qualifications for a traditional mortgage. If you've had a recent job change or are self-employed or have a high debt-to-income ratio, you may qualify for a non-QM. They do come with higher interest rates and fees, though.

The Federal Housing Authority, or FHA, also offers loans, and these are designed to help low- and middle-income borrowers qualify for a mortgage. They typically require a lower down payment and are more forgiving on credit score requirements. Reverse mortgages are a program under the FHA.

VA loans are guaranteed by the Department of Veterans Affairs and are available to eligible veterans, active-duty service members, and surviving spouses. No down payment is required, and their interest rates are competitive.

USDA loans are guaranteed by the US Department of Agriculture and are for low-income borrowers in rural areas. Like VA mortgages, they require no down payment and have low interest rates.

Though it's a multistep process that requires you to be realistic, qualifying for a mortgage may not be as overwhelming as you think. You can learn more about it in the next chapter.

3
QUALIFYING FOR A MORTGAGE

TAKE A DEEP BREATH AND LET IT OUT SLOWLY. Qualifying for a mortgage is probably a lot easier than you expect. Once again, part of my job as your mortgage broker is to walk you through the process.

The more you know up front, the easier it will be for you to become an aware buyer. Unpleasant surprises will not suddenly show up on your doorstep when you are properly prepared. In the examples I provide throughout this book, you can see how they might apply to you and how you can overcome potential obstacles on the way to getting a mortgage for your dream home.

We have a saying in my office: "Proper planning prevents poor performance." What this means is if you are adequately prepared for what is involved in securing a mortgage, the journey will be a lot easier and a lot less stressful for you.

However, if you just come sailing into any mortgage broker's office and expect them to secure a mortgage in three days or less when you have a 450 credit score on a home selling for $400,000, I hate to burst your bubble, but it's just not going to happen. Too often people hope they will be able to afford a specific home in a specific neighborhood. This is a fact of life, but hope is not a strategy. You must have a plan in place so you know what type of house and area you can afford to live in.

Being prepared before submitting a mortgage application does take some work and a little time. But I can help you with that. You won't be trying to do everything yourself. I'm here for you to help make everything easier.

Instead of going directly to a lender, go see a mortgage broker. An experienced mortgage broker will walk you through the entire process and make it as easy as possible. They will help you get into the best position to secure a mortgage loan for the home you desire.

HOW DO YOU QUALIFY FOR A MORTGAGE?

Getting preapproved for a mortgage is the first thing you should do before you even start looking at a home. Qualifying for a mortgage typically involves meeting certain criteria set by lenders. There isn't a one-size-fits-all, set-in-stone requirement. However, there are standard protocols used to determine whether you qualify for a mortgage. Lenders base their criteria on your credit score, your income, the type of property, and the specific type of mortgage you're applying for.

A real-life example involves Barbara and her partner of ten years, Ron. She has great credit. Ron, on the other hand, does not. When they came to see me, they were convinced that just because they had been together for ten years, had worked at their respective jobs for a number of years, and were making a decent income, they would automatically qualify for a mortgage loan at an outstanding rate.

After reviewing their financial situation, I knew Ron would not qualify for the mortgage. With his dismal credit score, there was no way they were going to receive a decent interest rate.

In many cases, one partner has a better credit rating than the other. One is typically more fiscally responsible than the other. This does affect the overall possibility of obtaining a mortgage together.

As I explained to them, lenders look at the items below to determine whether you're a good credit risk for a loan. You may have a great personality and be totally engaging, but lending institutions don't care about that. It's all about the numbers.

INCOME AND EMPLOYMENT

A stable employment history and proof of consistent income are crucial factors in determining whether you have the financial ability to repay the mortgage. As proof of income, they request copies of your tax returns, W-2s, bank statements, and possibly other financial documents.

Even in today's world of people constantly changing jobs, consistent employment history, especially with the same employer or in the same industry, positively impacts your mortgage application. In this case, both Barbara and Ron had worked at their respective jobs for a number of years. This was helpful information for the lenders.

Large employment gaps make lending institutions nervous. Remember, it's all about how likely you are to pay back the loan. Banks are very risk averse. They want to see stability and consistency in your life. They are not in the business of losing money. They are moneymakers, pure and simple. They want to know if you will pay them back.

In one sense, mortgage applicants are like that one family member who always seems to need money for their next idea, the one they are so sure is going to be the next big thing. No one in the family will ever have to worry about money ever again, they say. You may have even loaned money to them on occasion, thinking this may be the one time they actually hit it big. Chances are you've never been repaid, and you probably never will. There's always an excuse, and they are always the victim.

There's a downturn in the market. That big investor bailed out at the last minute. I decided I couldn't work with them. Name the excuse, and they've used it.

Now, ask yourself, "Would you loan them money for a house?" You would evaluate their past history of borrowing money and paying it back, their work history, and their income level. After you carefully consider everything you know about them, your answer is probably going to be no.

This is exactly what banks and credit unions go through when considering whether someone is a good credit risk or not. They want to be as reasonably sure as possible that they are going to be repaid for the mortgage loan.

Proving your income and employment is straight-forward if you work for someone else. But if you are self-employed, you will be asked to provide additional documentation for proof of income. You may have to submit your personal and business tax returns or business financial statements.

Danny was a self-employed electrician, recently divorced, with no kids, and wanted to buy a home. Not only did he have to submit his personal financial information, but he was also asked to provide copies of all his business tax returns and financial statements for the past two years to the lender. They required him to make a larger down payment on his purchase before they would approve his mortgage loan.

When you are self-employed, lenders are more cautious in lending because they know sales and income can fluctuate during the year. They want to be sure you can make the mortgage payments on time.

DEBT-TO-INCOME RATIO (DTI)

The debt-to-income ratio is what lenders use to compare your monthly debt payments to your gross monthly income (the amount you make before taxes come out). Don't stress! It's very easy to calculate, and you should know your DTI before ever applying for a mortgage loan.

For example, Barbara and Ron brought home approximately $70,000 after taxes or $5,833 per month between the two of them. Barbara had virtually no debt. She owed $500 on one credit card and that was it.

Ron's purchases of his new motorcycle, pontoon, and truck all contributed to his overall downfall of having a poor credit score since he was always juggling to make his payments and was often late on them. He was also reluctant to sell any of his toys and work on restoring his credit.

I explained the 46/56 rule to them. Basically, you need to know exactly how much of your gross monthly income goes toward housing expenses. It should be 46 percent or less. And you should be spending no more than 56 percent on your *total* debt. This includes housing and other payments, such as car loans and credit cards.

HOW DO YOU CALCULATE THESE PERCENTAGES?

Let's use Barbara and Ron's income as an example. Their gross income is approximately $91,000 per year, or $7,583 per month. Their net income (after taxes) is about $5,833 per month. They are currently paying $2,000 a month for rent, or $24,000 per year.

The easiest way to calculate the percentage is to multiply the gross income of $7,583 by 46 percent (0.46), which equals $3,488.

$$\$7,583 \times 0.46 = \$3,488$$

Their rent is $2,000 per month, so they are within the 46 percent rule. Good for them!

With Ron's history of poor credit payments, his monthly payments of $2,800 on his toys, and their net income of $5,833, a whopping 48 percent of their income is going to his bills. When you add their rent of $2,000 to Ron's $2,800, they are paying $4,800 per month when they are only bringing in $5,833. That leaves them with only $1,000 to pay for utilities, groceries, gas, lunches, eating out, and any miscellaneous items every month. That's not a lot. They simply aren't bringing in enough money to pay for everything. Lenders will not extend a mortgage offer on these numbers and after considering Ron's poor credit history.

Here's another example to help this really sink in: Juanita and Jose have a combined gross income of $80,000 a year, or $6,667 a month before taxes. Their current living expenses, including credit card debt, add up to $2,500 a month. To calculate their debt-to-income ratio, divide the $2,500 by $6,667, and you'll get 0.3749. (To convert this to a percentage, multiply it by 100, which gives 37 percent.) Some lenders will allow a debt-to-income ratio of up to 56 percent, but 46 percent or less is ideal.

A lower DTI ratio demonstrates your ability to manage your debt. Right now, only Barbara would qualify for a mortgage loan. Until Ron sells his motorcycle or pontoon and possibly gets an older car or pays off his bills, he won't be able to qualify for a loan. While Barbara could qualify for a loan based on her credit history and income, it would not be enough to qualify for the home they want.

Their dream of owning a home with a conventional mortgage is virtually nonexistent. You can see how one partner's spending habits can affect not only their own credit history but their partner's as well and can make owning a home together a very far-off dream.

Bluntly put, unless Barbara's income suddenly increases substantially, she and Ron will not be able to purchase a home just on her credit or on their credit together. And with his poor credit history, unless Ron sells his toys, he's not going to be able to contribute to the purchase of a home for the two of them. Even if he sells everything today, it will still take months for his poor financial choices to shake out on his credit scores.

Realistically, they are probably looking at a year before they can purchase a home if Ron decides to take responsibility for his purchases.

When one partner has impulsive spending habits, it can be extraordinarily difficult for them to change . . . and it won't happen overnight. Honestly, they may never change. Your dream of owning a home may not come to fruition without a lot of pain.

Can it be done? Yes. Will it be the house you really, truly want? Maybe not. Only you can decide what's more important to you: a home, or a partner you love who has disastrous spending habits.

Please note, I am not telling you to get rid of your partner. I just want to make you aware of the ramifications of their financial habits and how those can affect your present and future life together.

In this particular case, Barbara decided to take on a part-time job because she wanted a house she could call her own. She also loved Ron and wanted him to continue to be her partner. She realized he was probably not going to change his spending habits and it would be up to her to purchase a home for them.

She started driving DoorDash at night and on the weekends until she had saved enough money to make a nice down payment on the house she wanted. Was it easy? No. But once she had purchased the house, she said it was worth the journey. The long hours were worth her decision to buy a home. She was very proud of what she had accomplished.

Has Ron changed his spending habits? What do you think?

DOWN PAYMENT

A down payment is the amount of money you can put toward the purchase of your home on the day you buy it. A larger down payment reduces the loan-to-value ratio, or the amount you'll owe compared to the value of the home. It makes you a more attractive borrower to the lender.

For example, if Tina and Eddie put down 10 percent of the purchase price, they will rank higher than someone who has only 5 percent to put down. Both may still qualify for a mortgage, but the borrower who has the larger down payment will receive a better consideration on their loan interest rate.

Lending institutions will ask about the source of your down payment. In Tina and Eddie's case, they were both fresh out of college and had just started working in corporate America. They were also newly married.

Upon their return from their honeymoon, they were thrilled to learn that Tina's grandparents were going to give them $15,000 as a down payment on a townhome. Eddie's grandparents gave them another $15,000 for a down payment. They had a total of $30,000 to put down on their first home.

Their lending institution required both sets of grandparents to disclose the source of the large deposit. The lender wanted to be sure the grandparents weren't loaning the young couple the money for their new home. Basically, they didn't want Tina and Eddie to have a family loan payment in addition to the mortgage payment. They wanted to know that the couple would be able to make the payments on their own.

Young couples or young singles often receive money from a parent or grandparent for a down payment as a gift. Lenders typically require a family member to give money and not a friend.

OTHER FINANCIAL INFORMATION

Traditional lenders, such as banks and credit unions, may want to know how much is in your savings account, what type of financial reserves you have, and what your existing debts are. They may also consider the type of mortgage you're applying for (conventional, ARM, FHA, or VA).

If you decide to borrow from a family member or friend to purchase a home and bypass a lending institution, make sure you have an attorney draw up a contract between the two of you and you understand the terms of the agreement.

Keep in mind, when you use a private lender, they do not report your prompt payments to the credit reporting agencies. In one sense, you are hurting yourself by not establishing a good credit payment history.

You may also be taking financial risks that you aren't aware of initially. For example, Sally and her boyfriend Bobby wanted to buy a mobile home. They didn't qualify for a traditional mortgage, and they didn't have parents who could help them out financially.

There was a local gentleman, Russell, who made loans to individuals who couldn't get mortgages due to poor or nonexistent credit histories. Sally and Bobby were thrilled that this man was going to loan them the money for their new mobile home. They didn't have an attorney look over the agreement.

In fact, as they admitted to me later, they never even read the contract that was placed before them. They were so focused on getting the money for the mobile home, they never looked at the fine print.

What happened was a nightmare. Because they didn't read the contract, they didn't notice that they were paying double what the mobile home cost new. They didn't understand interest rates and how they could affect the mortgage payment amount. All they knew was they could afford the monthly payment Russell quoted them. They didn't even know that the interest rate they were paying was almost as high as what a credit card would charge on an unpaid balance.

They were to pay Russell in cash on the first day of every month at his office. Russell, being the slick individual that he was, had another little clause in the contract that stated he had to be paid in cash by a specific time on that day. If he was not paid by that time (and it was an odd time, like 11:17 a.m.), then a late penalty of fifty dollars would be added to the principal amount of the mortgage, and of course interest was accruing on the principal amount. He did not have to disclose to them that this late fee was being added to the principal.

After a year, Sally and Bobby came to see me. They thought that because they had been paying promptly on the first of each month, it was being reported to a credit reporting agency. It was not. They had been hoping to eventually qualify for a traditional mortgage and purchase a house instead of living in a double-wide mobile home.

Unfortunately, they did not have many good options. Their credit scores had improved over the course of a year, but with their income level and the spiraling prices of homes, it still wasn't enough for them to qualify for a home mortgage.

They were upside down on the value of their mobile home. Because they had not noticed their loan amount was double what the mobile home actually cost, there was no equity in the home. In fact, even though they were paying for it faithfully, mobile homes do not typically appreciate in value, and it was now worth far less than what they had paid for it.

I referred them to an attorney to see if he could help them with their situation. Also, please note, I am not saying all private lenders are shady and taking advantage of others. Had Sally and Bobby come to me, or any mortgage broker, we may have been able to find another way for them to get a mortgage.

Stories like this break my heart because I, and the mortgage brokers I know, want to help you obtain a loan so you can purchase your home. For us, it's not always about the numbers; it's about helping you get the home you desire.

PROPERTY APPRAISAL

Your potential lender may require an appraisal of the property you wish to purchase. The appraisal helps to ensure the loan amount aligns with the property's worth. In some instances, banks have loaned too much money for a home in a declining neighborhood. If you default on your mortgage, meaning you fail to pay it back, the lending institution will have a difficult time selling the property and getting the original loan amount back.

I experienced a situation early in my career when I was in the process of purchasing a home. Everything was on track for a successful closing until the bank sent out a property appraiser to evaluate the property's worth. The property's value did not come in as high as the purchase price, and they determined the house was not worth the loan amount. The seller did not agree with the appraisal, and the entire situation did not end well for me.

Lending institutions want to lend money on property that they believe will go up in value, but, more important than that, they want to be sure you can and will pay them back. And if something happens and you can't, if you go into foreclosure, they want to be sure they can sell the property for the amount they originally loaned you.

SPECIAL LENDER REQUIREMENTS

Besides the usual requirements, each lending institution has its own set of underwriting rules, procedures, and protocols to ensure they make a wise decision about giving you a mortgage loan.

This is where a mortgage broker's expertise is invaluable to you. We know the local area, the right lenders to approach for your loan, and ways to make the process as easy as possible for you.

When you select a mortgage broker, you want someone who has a wide range of experience with the different mortgage products, is knowledgeable about which lending institution is likely to be best for you, and can help you through the entire process of securing a mortgage.

CREDIT SCORES

Your credit score is critical. Banks, credit unions, and other lenders will review your credit history and score. This is also known as a FICO score. FICO stands for Fair Isaac Corporation. The higher your credit score, the better the chance you'll receive a much lower interest rate.

If you plan to make only a minimum down payment, your credit score needs to be at least 580, and some lenders require a higher score depending on the type of mortgage you're seeking and your credit history. In this case, Barbara's credit score was substantially better than her partner's, which made her a better credit risk for a mortgage. Just because a couple has been together for years does not necessarily make the both of them excellent credit risks for a lending institution.

Lending institutions have their own criteria for mortgage loans. Regardless of the bank, credit union, or other institution you go to, every one of them will use all of the following credit reporting agencies to get your financial history.

The top three credit reporting agencies are TransUnion, Equifax, and Experian. While they all use slightly different methods of calculating your credit score, it's important to have an idea of what your credit score is prior to applying for a mortgage. I've listed these agencies' contact information in the Resources section.

How do credit reporting agencies produce your score? They use a number of different factors and mathematical algorithms. The key component is your payment history. Making on-time payments is a crucial factor. Consistently paying your bills by the due date helps establish a positive credit history, while late or missed payments can have a negative impact.

Although you may be making your payments, if they are consistently late, this negatively impacts your credit rating. It's one of the most overlooked financial pieces of information you need to set yourself up for success.

If you need to, write down when your bills are due on a calendar with the dollar amount. Place it where you are going to see it on a daily basis. Put it on your refrigerator or tape it to a wall. Set yourself up for success.

It may seem simple and not that important, but the difference between paying your bills on time and being a day or two late can affect your credit score by as much as twenty points. Those twenty points may decide whether you can just secure a mortgage or secure a mortgage with a lower interest rate.

Something else lending institutions and credit reporting agencies use is the credit utilization ratio. This number compares the amount of credit you're currently using to the total credit available to you. Ideally, you should keep the amount you owe on a credit card below 30 percent of what is available to you.

What does this really mean to you? If you have Credit Card A with a spending limit of $2,500 and Credit Card B with a limit of $3,000, you will probably assume your current balance of $1,650 falls within that 30 percent. It does, based on the total amount; however, if you have outstanding balances of $2,000 on Credit Card A and $2,650 on Credit Card B, you're no longer under 30 percent, and this could well impact your score.

With a balance of $2,000 on Credit Card A, you are over the 50 percent ratio, and this will hinder your credit score and could make banks rather hesitant to view your outstanding balance in a positive light. They tend to think perhaps you're not a good money manager. Remember, they are very risk averse and are therefore very conservative when it comes to loaning money.

There's an old cliché: "Banks only loan money to people who don't need it." It can certainly feel that way. It's almost like lending institutions are looking for a reason not to give you a mortgage loan.

You, on the other hand, want to play the game to win—that is, to receive the loan.

When you keep your credit utilization ratio to 30 percent or less, this demonstrates responsible credit management to a lender. Keep in mind, the average American has four credit cards and $8,000 in credit card debt. While this makes credit card companies very happy, it doesn't inspire confidence in a mortgage lender. What can create that confidence is a long credit history with specific lenders because it provides a more comprehensive picture of your creditworthiness.

For example, if Roberta has been making her car payments on time for the past three years, she will be favored more in credit scoring than someone who has only been making car payments for twelve months.

When you have a diverse mix of credit accounts, such as credit cards, mortgages, auto loans or student loans, they can positively impact your score. It demonstrates your ability to handle different types of credit responsibly. Again, making your payments on time makes a big difference in your credit scores.

Laneetha has three credit cards, a car loan, and a student loan she has been making payments on for the past four years. She has a dependable job, and she makes all of her payments on time. She is an excellent candidate for a mortgage loan.

Jordan also has three credit cards, a car loan, and a student loan. Her credit cards are maxed out, and she's often late with her car payment and her student loan. It would be very tough for her to get a mortgage. It's not impossible, but it would be tough, and she would probably be paying more with higher interest rates.

Remember, a few minutes ago, when I said you want to keep your credit card usage within 30 percent of your available credit? Besides not using credit cards too much, opening too many credit card accounts in a short period of time can wave red flags with a lending institution. Different institutions use various qualifiers to evaluate your financial stability. Having six credit cards with some type of balance on each one or receiving several new cards within a short time makes lending institutions wonder why you have a sudden need for credit. They may start examining your credit history with a fine-tooth comb or they may call in another more conservative qualifier to determine whether you meet their criteria as a good credit risk for a mortgage.

Anytime you submit a mortgage loan application, you want to stack the odds in your favor as much as possible. You may think you're being responsible by having umpteen credit cards, but in a lender's eyes, it makes you highly suspect of credit mismanagement.

Far too many people are tempted to spend once they receive a new credit card. It almost seems like free money, especially since you don't have to pay it back all at one time. You can make minimum payments for the rest of your life. It's too easy and too tempting for many people. But if they would just keep the card as an emergency backup measure, it would help their credit scores and eliminate a lot of stress down the road when they find they no longer have credit available on that card or when they can't make their payments.

With bankruptcies on the rise, lending institutions don't want to be put in the situation of loaning money to you, then finding out you're filing Chapter 13 or Chapter 7.

Also, many people are unaware that when you complete a credit application, it typically results in a hard inquiry on your credit report. This new inquiry can temporarily lower your credit score, which is why your credit score can vary by several points every time you check it.

Credit reporting agencies pull information from public records, which includes bankruptcies, tax liens, foreclosures, vehicle repossessions, and collections. These have a significant negative impact on your credit score.

Negative scores can stay on your credit report for seven years, in some cases up to ten years. They can directly impact your insurance rates and where you can rent a home or apartment. They can even cause you not to be able to own a home by getting a mortgage through traditional lenders.

Anything you do from a financial standpoint will show up at some point through the credit reporting agencies, so it pays to check your credit score on a regular basis. Sometimes a bill or charge may show up that has absolutely nothing to do with you, or a paid-off bill may suddenly appear and show that it is still open.

Karla saw this happen several months after her husband died. Charges that she knew nothing about suddenly showed up on her credit report, including a bill that she and her husband had paid off over five years earlier.

How did she find out about these charges? She received a free copy of her credit report. Anyone can receive one once a year, every twelve months, from TransUnion, Experian, and Equifax by going to AnnualCreditReport. com. You may also check your credit scores for free whenever you want by setting up a free account at CreditKarma.com.

Karla immediately filed a report with each of the agencies to dispute the new charges, provided proof that she and her husband had paid the bill in question, and checked every week to see what her credit score was and whether the offending charges had been deleted from her report. It took several months to get it rectified, but she was able to have everything inaccurate removed.

Ignoring your credit scores can have a devastating effect on other bills in your life, not just on your ability to obtain a mortgage. For example, your car insurance rates could be higher, your credit card interest rates could increase, or you could be turned down for a new credit card. You could also be denied approval for a new apartment or be required to put down a substantial deposit. It could affect your employment or the type of job you can get.

Conversely, paying for everything in cash can also have a negative effect on your credit score. If you never use credit, lenders have nothing to base your creditworthiness on. It's almost like you're being penalized for being a wise money handler.

Also, if you have lived out of the country for a period of time and then come back to the United States, it is like starting all over again with building a credit history.

Melissa and Oliver lived in Hong Kong for over ten years. He was an executive with a large international company. He was offered the opportunity to come back to the United States with a big promotion and a large increase in salary. They both jumped at the chance to come back and make a new home.

They came to see me hoping to streamline the process of purchasing a home. Surprisingly, it took a little longer to get them approved for a mortgage even though they had a substantial down payment and Oliver had a great salary with a company he had been with for ten years.

However, for all practical purposes, they didn't have any personal credit history. Everything they had purchased in Hong Kong was paid for on his company credit card or through his expense report. When they traveled to the US, everything was paid for through Oliver's company.

It was a bit of a challenge to get them approved for a mortgage, and the interest rate was a little high. Melissa and Oliver agreed it was more important for them to get into a home than to worry about the interest rate at that time. As I pointed out to them, we could always restructure the mortgage in two to three years. They were happy with that.

WHY NOT TO USE CREDIT REPAIR COMPANIES

Other than your mother, no one is going to love you like you do. Bluntly put, credit repair companies do not have any skin in the game. They don't have to ensure that what they say they are doing will actually improve your credit score.

They will promise to "fix" late payment notices, bankruptcy, judgments against you, charge-offs, foreclosures, vehicle repossessions, collections, and hard inquiries.

What do they really do? They request your credit report from TransUnion, Equifax, and Experian. They can submit a reduced payment plan to your creditors, with no guarantee that any creditor will agree to a lesser amount than what you owe.

They may use illicit or slick tactics to get you, the customer, to comply with what they want. Again, there's no guarantee that they will actually do what they promise or that they can fix your financial problems. They are allegedly making the effort to contact your credit card companies and other companies you owe money to.

Here's the kicker: over 36 percent of all complaints about credit repair companies are traced back to outright consumer fraud and scams, according to the Consumer Financial Protection Bureau. In fact, scams and consumer fraud are so high in this industry that many traditional merchant payment processors refuse to offer merchant account services to credit repair companies.

What do the complaints about credit repair companies typically center on? Deceitful advertising, missing disclosures, unnecessary costs, hidden fees, and nonexistent customer service are just a few of the many complaints lodged against this industry.

Still not convinced about credit repair companies? Try this on for size: they offer high ticket services starting at one hundred dollars, they add extra fees without explaining those fees to you, they attempt to force you into a subscription plan "so you won't have these problems again," and they leave fraudulent charges on your credit or debit card. They are high-pressure salespeople.

You can actually do the exact same thing the credit repair companies do to fix and/or dispute your credit score, but for no cost.

Helena and Ralph came to me because they needed help securing a mortgage loan. Helena was shocked when she checked her credit score and discovered it was less than stellar. There were charges on her report that had been paid off for several years but were still listed, and several new credit cards were listed that she had never ordered or received.

She had seen several TV commercials about credit repair. She called one of the repair companies and paid them several hundred dollars to have the old credit card charges deleted from her account and the new credit cards removed from her report.

Helena checked her scores once a week, and after the first month she called the credit repair company. She was told that it would take sixty days for any changes to show up on her report but that they were on top of things. Months 2 and 3 went by with no changes on her credit report.

During month 4, she and Ralph came to me because they were trying to get their mortgage approved. After she explained all of the above to me, I suggested she contact each of the three credit reporting agencies and find out if anything had ever been submitted to them regarding her credit cards. She submitted a request to each of them and was told no disputes were ever filed on her behalf.

To say Helena was livid was an understatement, according to her husband Ralph. I told her to dispute everything with the credit reporting agencies. She completed everything needed for TransUnion, Equifax, and Experian that day to dispute the charges. She also called the credit repair company and demanded her money back. Unfortunately, if you look at the very fine print, you will see that credit repair companies don't guarantee any results, and most do not refund money.

She continued to check her scores weekly and waited for the appropriate time for each of the credit reporting agencies to respond to her dispute—usually fourteen business days. Then she followed up with the agencies, and within sixty days she had everything resolved. All of the old credit card charges were removed. The new credit cards that she had known nothing about were also deleted from her account. She had contacted the issuing credit card companies to explain that the cards were not hers and had been obtained fraudulently, and all of that was removed as well. We were able to help Helena and Ralph get the mortgage loan for their new home.

If you've had credit issues and it has negatively affected your credit scores, make every effort on your own to do your own credit repair. Do not spend hundreds of dollars with a so-called credit repair company when you can do it all yourself.

Keep in mind, if you use a credit repair company, the credit reporting agencies are going to need to talk with you anyway. You could spend that same amount of time contacting the credit reporting agencies yourself to dispute the charges.

How? You can dispute any error on your credit report by contacting each of the three main credit reporting agencies online.

It couldn't be easier with the internet. You don't even have to make a telephone call, wait forever on hold, and pull your hair out. Completing the dispute forms online will literally take you less than ten minutes. The agencies respond fairly quickly to disputes, and they may ask you to submit additional documentation or information. Realistically, it will take you several weeks to several months to dispute inaccurate charges, and you may need to submit documentation or information several times before they are deleted from your account.

If there are any hard inquiries to your credit report during the time you are disputing everything, there will be a notification stating that. If the charges cannot be removed or reduced from your credit report, contact the lender directly. Be sure to get the name of the person you speak with and write down the date and time when you call to dispute the charges.

If the disputed charges are legitimate, they will stay on your credit report. You will not be able to remove bankruptcies or foreclosures. They can stay on your credit record for as long as ten years.

Instead of beating yourself up for your poor financial habits or choices, resolve to make better choices in the future. What can you do today to start building a good credit history? Don't laugh, but building good credit is really about changing your mindset to go after what you want.

I help people all the time to get mortgage loans for the house they've always wanted. I'll let you in on a secret: It's not about getting things. It's about creating and getting the emotion you want.

You want a mortgage loan for a house, your own home, so you can feel proud of yourself, secure, like you're building a future because your home will build equity.

It really comes down to this: thoughts are the currency you use to purchase your dreams. Don't let old, bad financial habits keep you from your dream of owning your own home. You can do it by changing your mindset.

How do you start improving your credit score? Get a secured credit card. Most banks have a secured credit card that you can put two hundred dollars or more on, and that's your credit limit. They report to the credit agencies once a month. If you spend no more than 20 percent of the card's limit and pay it off each month, your score will go up. It may happen slowly, but it will go up.

So, in conclusion, credit repair companies cannot do anything for you that you cannot do for yourself. Be mindful and careful when you consider working with one.

4
The Hidden Costs

WHEN TOMMY AND TEMEKA first came to me, they had found a home they thought they could afford. As I explained the mortgage loan process, they were beyond shocked at the hidden costs of actually purchasing a home. That's why a mortgage broker is invaluable to you from the beginning of your journey of buying a home.

Knowing what all your costs are going to be when the deal is closed helps you avoid sticker shock and a broken pocketbook or wallet. Your down payment is not the only thing needed when you head to your closing. It is a disservice to you for someone not to explain all the costs of the closing of your new home.

Closing on your home can be stress-inducing in general. Why? Because, for most people, this is the single biggest purchase they will ever make in their life, and there are a lot of emotions involved.

The last thing you want is to discover you need several thousand dollars more at the last second and to have to figure out where you're going to get that money. You've made it this far, and you don't want to have everything fall apart at the last minute because you didn't know exactly what was needed.

I do everything possible to make sure this never happens to you. I made Tommy and Temeka aware of the closing costs so they could prepare well in advance and have what they needed. I want to make you aware, so you are an informed consumer.

CLOSING COSTS

Closing costs typically run between 2 and 6 percent of the total purchase price of the home. For example, on a $350,000 home, the closing costs could range from $7,000 to $21,000. Sellers can incentivize buyers to purchase by offering to pay most of the closing costs, but that is on a case-by-case basis.

What are the closing costs? They are the expenses incurred during the process of buying or selling a home. They are typically paid at the closing of the real estate transaction and cover lender fees, title fees and the cost of setting up an escrow account. Here's a formula for the money you actually bring to the table at closing:

(Down Payment + Closing Costs) - (Earnest Money
+ Real Estate Tax Prorations) + Seller Credits

DOWN PAYMENT

As we discussed in a previous chapter, mortgages usually require a down payment, which typically ranges from 3 to 35 percent of the property's purchase price, depending on the program.

After you've made an offer on a home and before it closes, you may have to have a home inspection done. These fees range from $250 up, with an average cost of approximately $375. Make sure you use a licensed home inspector.

The American Society of Home Inspectors (HomeInspectors.org) is a national association that requires its members to be certified. Your brother-in-law who works in construction should not be the person inspecting your home.

Home inspectors assess the condition of residential properties. They conduct thorough inspections to identify any existing or potential issues with the structure, systems, and components of a home. They examine its foundation, walls, floors, roof, and overall structural integrity. They look for signs of cracks, settlement, water damage, or other issues that could affect the livability and stability of the property.

They also inspect the exterior walls, siding, windows, doors, decks, balconies, porches, and driveways. They look for any damage, deterioration, or safety hazards.

Inspectors assess the condition of the roof, including the materials, flashing, gutters, and downspouts. They check for leaks, damaged shingles, or signs of inadequate maintenance.

They examine the plumbing system, including supply lines, drainage, and fixtures. Inspectors check for leaks, water pressure issues, faulty pipes, and proper functioning of toilets, sinks, showers, and bathtubs.

The home inspector evaluates the electrical system, including the main panel, wiring, outlets, switches, and fixtures. They check for code compliance, potential safety hazards, and the presence of grounding and proper circuit protection.

They look at the HVAC (heating, ventilation, and air conditioning), including furnaces, air conditioners, heat pumps, ductwork, and thermostats. The home inspector checks for proper operation, maintenance, and potential energy efficiency concerns.

They also evaluate the insulation levels in the walls, attic, and crawl spaces. They assess ventilation systems to ensure there is proper airflow and no mold or excessive moisture.

Most home inspectors also check major appliances, such as ovens, stoves, dishwashers, refrigerators, and laundry machines, to ensure they are functioning correctly.

If your prospective new home has safety features, such as smoke detectors, carbon monoxide detectors, handrails, and guardrails, they will be checked as well.

After completing the inspection, the home inspector provides a detailed report outlining their findings, including any defects, deficiencies, or recommended repairs or maintenance tasks.

If improvements need to be made, they can be negotiated with the seller of the home. If the owner does not want to make the repairs or provide you with a seller credit, you may want to choose another house.

Older homes typically need repairs. Only you can decide whether you want the home and if it's worth doing the repairs yourself.

Again, a home inspection should be completed within five business days of your offer being accepted on the property you want to purchase. It can provide peace of mind, so you know exactly what you're purchasing.

HOME APPRAISAL

Your lender may require an appraisal to confirm the market value of the home. The difference between a home inspection and a home appraisal is that the appraisal establishes a fair market value for the property, while a home inspection identifies and makes a potential buyer aware of potential problems with the house. In some cases, an appraiser may point out safety and hazard concerns, but appraisers tend to be less thorough than home inspectors since their main objective is to ensure the market value supports the purchase contract in a transaction.

The lender will require the appraisal to be conducted by a licensed appraiser. The lender wants to make sure the property is worth the selling price so they can determine the amount of financing to offer. This also helps both the buyer and seller to know the worth of the home.

Jane and Harry may want to sell their home for $300,000, but Ted and Alice's lender will conduct an appraisal to determine the market value of the home. The lender, after receiving the appraiser's report, may decide to lend only $250,000 for the mortgage if the value comes in at only $275,000. The appraisal is a very important part of the transaction for all parties involved.

What does the appraiser evaluate? They look at the overall condition of the home, including its age, size, and any amenities or renovations. They evaluate specific features, such as the number of bedrooms and bathrooms, the layout, the quality of construction, and any unique characteristics.

They also analyze recent sales of similar properties in the area to determine how the subject property compares in terms of size, features, and location. Typically, a comparable of the subject property needs to be within a one-mile radius. A very important consideration for the lender is the current market condition, the neighborhood, and the property value trends in that area. They want to know if the property values are trending up or down in the neighborhood.

The appraiser takes all these factors into consideration and then provides the lender with a detailed appraisal report estimating the property's value. The appraisal process and the time it takes may vary depending on the location and specific requirements of the lender. It may take several weeks.

Sometimes buyers are expected to pay the appraisal fee up front. Generally, home appraisal costs can range from $475 to $1,050, depending on the urgency of return of the appraisal and the type of property.

ESCROW FEES

The title company, also known as an escrow company, acts as a neutral third party that holds and distributes funds, documents, and other assets on behalf of the buyer and seller to ensure a smooth and secure transfer of property. It provides the checks and balances needed in a real estate transaction so that everything is fair, aboveboard, and equitable for everyone involved. The escrow company acts as a neutral intermediary, holding funds and documents until all the necessary conditions of the transaction are met.

Escrow fees can cover a range of services provided by the escrow company or attorney. These services may include handling the earnest money deposit, verifying the title, coordinating the transfer of funds, preparing necessary legal documents, and ensuring that all conditions outlined in the purchase agreement are met before the closing.

Who pays for the escrow fees? About three-fourths of the time, both sides pay—the buyer and seller split the fees. In other cases, they negotiate payment by one side, usually the buyer. The allocation of fees can be specified in the purchase agreement or negotiated during the transaction.

TITLE INSURANCE

The lender also requires title insurance. This is one of the variables in how much money you will need to bring at closing. Generally, the real estate agents or attorneys choose the title company that will be closing the deal, and each title company has its own set of fees that are incorporated into your closing costs.

Here's what happened to Robin, an eight-year, honorably discharged US Marine. She had seen a low-priced home on a flier at the grocery store, and she contacted the owner. She bought the house with cash from the seller without ordering a copy of the title.

She moved her disabled, elderly grandparents and her ten-year-old grandson into her new home. Six months later, there was a knock at the door, and a lady told her that she had been in Europe for the past eight months but that this was her home and Robin needed to move out as soon as possible.

This became a very sticky situation. Law enforcement was called, and Robin, her grandparents, and her grandson were evicted. Robin showed them all her documentation, which in her mind proved that she owned the property.

It turned out that the individual who had "sold" her the property had carried out the same scam on a number of other people and was wanted in multiple counties for fraud.

Robin came to me, not knowing what to do. She was in a desperate situation with a very short time frame. She wanted and needed a home for her family. She worked full-time and still cared for her grandparents and grandson, so her funds were very limited.

Luckily, she had found another home, but she didn't know how to get a mortgage. She was referred to me by a previous client who told me her crazy story. I found a VA (Veterans Administration) program to help get her into a new home, and the rest is history.

Without a title commitment, you might not know who actually owns the house or find out about a title defect, such as a prior recorded mortgage, a judgment, or a tax lien. These kinds of debts have to be satisfied prior to the closing of your home. There could also be an environmental lien, a notice of pending legal action, an easement, or some type of restriction. This information might appear only in a title insurance search.

If you don't have title insurance, someone could show up with a tax lien on your new home, and theoretically they could own it. Title insurance is very important and is a relatively small price to pay for peace of mind. The cost ranges from .05 to 2 percent of the home's purchase price. Title insurance protects both you and the lender. It protects you, the buyer, against loss or damage to the title. You don't want to end up like Robin, evicted from what she thought was her home and out of all the money she had paid, because you didn't have title insurance to confirm ownership.

MORTGAGE INSURANCE

Mortgage insurance, or private mortgage insurance (PMI), protects the lender if you default on your mortgage. If you make less than a 20 percent down payment on your new home, mortgage insurance will be required. If you are getting an FHA or USDA loan, it will be required.

Why is mortgage insurance required if you have less than a 20 percent down payment? Because a lower down payment represents a higher risk for the lender. The mortgage insurance helps protect the lender against potential losses. It lowers the risk of making you the loan. If you default on the loan and the property goes into foreclosure, the mortgage insurance reimburses the lender for the losses.

But it also increases the cost of your loan. Typically, the borrower pays the mortgage insurance premiums as part of their monthly mortgage payment. The amount of the premium varies depending on the loan-to-value ratio, the creditworthiness of the borrower, and the specific mortgage insurance provider.

The good news about mortgage insurance: once your equity in your home reaches 20 percent, you can refinance to remove the PMI from your monthly payment. On a conventional loan, once you reach a 78 percent loan-to-value ratio based on your purchase price, assuming you never refinance, you are eligible to request the cancellation of mortgage insurance. Some other products, like FHA loans, have specific time frames before the insurance can be removed.

Note that mortgage insurance protects the lender and not you. It does not provide any direct benefit to the homeowner, aside from allowing them to qualify for a mortgage with a lower down payment. Your mortgage broker will be able to explain what is required in your particular mortgage.

HOMEOWNERS ASSOCIATION FEES

If you are purchasing a home that has a homeowners association (HOA), you may need to pay those fees up front, or there may be an initiation fee. The HOA may require a year's fee in advance, or you may need to pay the arrears of the previous owner who failed to make payments to the association at the time of closing.

What are HOA fees? They are recurring fees charged by a homeowner's association to cover costs associated with the management, maintenance, and operation of common areas and amenities within the community. Typically, HOA fees cover landscaping, security, trash removal, snow removal, common area repairs, insurance for common areas, and administration costs.

The HOA typically develops a projected annual budget, then divides the total expenses among the homeowners on a monthly, quarterly, or sometimes annual basis. It depends on how the HOA bylaws are written. HOA fees can vary greatly depending on the size of the community, the amenities offered, and the level of maintenance required. Be aware, HOA fees can also increase significantly over time due to rising costs or major repairs to common buildings.

If you live in an HOA community, the fees are mandatory for all homeowners, and nonpayment can lead to penalties or legal action by the HOA. You or your attorney should carefully review the HOA's rules and regulations, paying close attention to their policies on fee payment and any penalties or late fees associated with nonpayment.

Homeowners are entitled to review the HOA's budget and financial statements to understand how their fees are being used. This transparency allows homeowners to assess whether the HOA's financial management aligns with their expectations.

Before purchasing a property in an HOA-governed community, it's important to carefully consider the associated HOA fees in your budget and financial planning. Remember, these fees never go down and can increase substantially over the years. The HOA dues are a separate payment from the mortgage, but they are still factored into the debt-to-income ratio when determining what loans a borrower can qualify for.

TRANSFER TAX

Depending on your state, you might also have to pay a transfer tax, which is collected by your state or local government office. A transfer tax essentially covers the cost of passing the title from the seller to the buyer and is sometimes called a deed transfer tax or a real estate transfer tax.

Who pays the transfer tax? It depends. In some states, the seller is responsible for paying the transfer tax.

In other states, it may be split between the buyer and seller, or it may be paid only by the buyer.

How is the transfer tax calculated? Typically, it is calculated as a percentage of the property's sale price. Just as a heads-up, the transfer tax rate can vary widely. It can range from a fraction of a percent to several percentage points. Your mortgage broker should be able to provide the information.

The transfer tax is collected at the time of closing, along with other closing costs. The escrow company or real estate attorney makes sure that the appropriate amount is paid to the government.

OTHER COSTS

Typically, a credit report fee will be charged at closing. The lender needs to see your credit report to assess your creditworthiness.

Depending on your lender, you may be able to pay a discount fee point up front to lower the interest rate on your mortgage.

Owner's title insurance is optional, but it does protect your interest in the property.

There will be recording fees for recording the new deed and other legal documents with the county in which the property resides.

YOUR MORTGAGE BROKER

As a mortgage broker, I may be able to have the lender waive or reduce the origination fee and some of the other costs associated with a real estate closing. Mortgage brokers generally have access to a broader assortment of products and programs than lenders do.

Part of my job is to do the math and tell you what size mortgage you can qualify for. I do research on mortgage rates and fees. I can negotiate the fees and keep the mortgage process on track. As your mortgage broker, I will make you aware of all expenses up front. I don't like sudden financial surprises, either, and I want to ensure you are aware of all expenses.

According to the Consumer Financial Protection Bureau, almost half of homebuyers don't shop around before applying for a mortgage. If you're in that group (and hopefully you won't be now), you'll probably leave a lot of money on the table because you don't understand all the nuances of the mortgage process.

Interest rates may fluctuate from lender to lender. There could be a gap of 0.5 percent between the lenders' interest rates. The interest rates depend on your credit score and the loan program you choose. Generally speaking, lenders have overhead costs for their retail offices and have to bake the costs in by charging higher interest rates. That can add up to thousands of dollars over the course of your mortgage loan.

As a mortgage broker, I can help you avoid the pitfalls because I know the mortgage industry. I know the differences between the various lenders and the many twists and turns in the mortgage process, so I can help you shop around for the best products, programs, and interest rates. Mortgage brokers provide wholesale pricing instead of retail pricing.

If you have a tricky financial situation—maybe your credit history isn't great or the property you're buying is unusual—a mortgage broker can find a lender who has more flexibility with credit scores and down payment amounts or who specializes in certain types of properties.

From finding the best interest rate and lowest fees to completing the application and closing the loan on time, we mortgage brokers are well versed in the process of getting a mortgage. Working with a mortgage broker to navigate today's market is a wise move, especially for a first-time homebuyer.

"A mortgage broker not only helps you get the most competitive rates and pricing, but also helps make sure your loan is a good match with the particular lender," explains Andrew Weinberg, principal at Silver Fin Capital Group in Great Neck, New York. "They can quickly determine the best lender for each individual borrower."

Lower the stress in your life by letting a mortgage broker do all the paperwork for you.

SUMMARY

As you can see, all these hidden costs can add up in a hurry. Most people, including Tommy and Temeka, severely underestimate how much money they actually need in addition to the down payment on their home.

This is where a good mortgage broker can help prepare you in advance and guide you through the steps of securing a mortgage loan.

5
AFFORDING WHAT YOU WANT

YOU LOVE THE EXCLUSIVE GATED COMMUNITY
with the guard, the beautifully manicured lawns, and the
clubhouse, gym, golf course, and tennis courts. That's what
you want, and that's what your heart desires. However . . .

Can you afford the type of home you want in the
neighborhood you want on your current income? As harsh
as this may sound, hope is not a strategy. The numbers
have to work in your favor for you to be able to afford
what you want. It's not enough to think you might be
able to afford to live in a specific area when the numbers
just don't work.

It's an exercise in futility to run to a mortgage broker
and demand they find a way for you to obtain a mortgage
so you can live in a specific neighborhood if you don't
make enough money, your credit score is in the low 500s,
and you have a habit of working for a couple of months
and then taking off a month. Mortgage brokers can do a

lot of things for our clients; however, we cannot wave a magic wand and make poor financial choices disappear.

You do have to be realistic about what you can and can't afford. Are you willing to work two jobs, clean up your credit score, and make the necessary changes in your life to afford that particular home? Now is the time to be offensive minded. Don't give up on your dream home. Be proactive. Think strategy.

I'll go out on a limb here and say maybe living in that particular neighborhood isn't really what you want. Perhaps you think you have to have that kind of house, have to live in that kind of area, or have to be that kind of person to be successful.

There is a lot of psychology involved in the purchase of a home. It's not just about making the numbers work or choosing a cute brick-and-mortar or other style of home. As an experienced mortgage broker, I have seen couples come into my office and say one thing while their actions indicate something else.

Susan and Gary were looking at a ritzy home in a prestigious neighborhood. Gary was very boisterous, stating this was the type of home and area he wanted to live in. He just knew he'd be the envy of his family. He had finally made it to the big time. His siblings would all be jealous of him.

Susan was a little bit more subdued than her husband. However, her attitude was along the same lines as Gary's: they would "show family" how well they were now doing.

I listened and observed what they were saying. Something was off. It was around the noon hour, and I suggested we go grab a bite to eat. I asked them where their favorite place to eat was, and I admit I was thinking it was going to be an upscale restaurant. I was shocked when they said McDonald's and told me they ate there a couple of times a week.

There was the little something I had not been able to put my finger on. What they were saying they wanted was incongruent with their everyday actions. They would not be happy in that gated community.

I wanted to help them get a mortgage in an area where they could truly be happy. It seemed like they were chasing the dream of others. I needed to ask them some hard questions.

Keep in mind, there are so many emotions involved in the purchase of a home. Surprisingly, many people never take the time to evaluate what they really want in a lifestyle, and let's face it—a lifestyle is what you're purchasing when you buy a home.

In fact, let's really break it down. Have you ever asked yourself what type of lifestyle you truly want to live? Not how family members think you should live, and not based on the opinions of friends who question why you don't have the same type of lavish home they do.

Let me toss out a thought that you may have never considered. Maybe, just maybe, you could be happy with something different. Perhaps you "want" a lavish lifestyle and a very nice, luxurious home but don't really believe you deserve it.

Knowing and deciding on the type of lifestyle you want prior to looking for a home will save you a lot of angst. Too many people look at what they can afford, ignore the lifestyle part, and end up unhappy in a neighborhood they truly never wanted to be in.

Another true-life example of this is Karen and Bill. Both had been married and divorced before marrying each other. Bill was the primary breadwinner and wanted to buy a home out in the country where the closest neighbor was over a mile away.

Karen also wanted a country home; however, she didn't want to be that far away from neighbors in case of a natural disaster, an accident, or a medical emergency. She wanted to be able to look out her kitchen window and see another home within walking distance.

Their new joint home was creating a lot of problems between them. They were actually on the verge of divorce when they came to see me. Why, since I'm not a marriage counselor? Because they had each agreed they would need a new home, and they each needed a mortgage broker.

After discovering what each of them wanted in a home and, more importantly, what was essential for them to have the lifestyle they both wanted, I could help them both achieve the lifestyle they wanted while keeping their marriage intact.

Is it normal for a mortgage broker to do this? Sometimes, when we truly want to help someone secure a mortgage for the home of their dreams. Lifestyle involves introspection and self-awareness as well as other factors that influence your well-being and values.

Because their realtor had never asked either of them the lifestyle question, Bill and Karen had ended up buying a home they physically liked but had never considered how it would affect their day-to-day living. Karen felt isolated and unhappy because she couldn't see any neighbors. Bill was unhappy because Karen was unhappy, but he was unwilling to entertain the thought of moving a little closer to town.

Listening to them bicker, I realized they really just needed some guidance on what they both wanted and needed so they could find a neighborhood where they would both be happy.

As I pointed out to the two of them, the psychology of buying a home involves both the emotions and cognitive factors. It influences the decision-making process and overall experience of purchasing a property. Yes, the numbers have to work, but a home represents more than just a physical structure. Particularly for women, it's often associated with the emotions of comfort, security, and personal identity.

People may develop an emotional attachment to a particular property or envision it as a place to create memories and build a sense of belonging, which is what Susan and Gary were looking for.

For some people, the process of searching for a home and envisioning what can be done to the home to create the type of environment they want is more fun than the actual purchase.

Gary admitted to me on the side that he was very anxious about the significant financial commitment he was going to have to make if he and Susan were going to purchase that particular home. He was afraid of making the wrong choice. He was concerned that if something happened to his job, they would not be able to afford the home, and the embarrassment of losing it would be catastrophic to his ego.

He was trying to be rational in the decision-making process, but his emotions were still trying to take over.

I explained to him that the numbers were rational. Could they afford the home on just one salary if something happened to his job? The answer was no. Did they have enough savings to live on for six months? Again, the answer was no.

Coming back together with Susan, I wanted to know what a home—note I used the word *home* and not *house*—meant to her. What was important to her about owning a home?

She wanted to be in an affluent neighborhood where she could also have social connections. She wanted a sense of pride, and Gary wanted a sense of accomplishment. It represented a significant milestone and achievement for him.

The thought may have occurred to you that this couple has low self-esteem, and they were trying to use the purchase of a home in an upscale gated community to bolster their self-confidence. Maybe yes, maybe no.

Understanding the psychology of my clients makes it much easier to help them secure a mortgage on the home they want. Yes, my job as a mortgage broker is to run the numbers and help you get a loan, but securing a loan is only considering a small part of your life.

If I help you get the loan, but you end up hating the neighborhood, then you're going to blame both me and the realtor. You also won't think positively of me when you want to purchase another home. I like having long-term relationships with my clients.

When you and your partner know the exact type of lifestyle you want to live, it makes choosing a home and a neighborhood easier.

Karen and Bill had a different situation. Because they had not discussed what they wanted in a house and neighborhood, it created buyer's remorse, which led to hard feelings between them.

After I went over the lifestyle questions with them, they understood what it would take to make both of them happy. After six months, they did find an area they thought they could both be happy in, and I was able to quickly process the mortgage loan paperwork for them. They are still married.

Let's look at another couple, Greg and Liz. Greg was an auto mechanic, and Liz was a secretary. They lived in a modest home in a lower-middle-class neighborhood, drove a paid-off car and truck, didn't eat out much, and preferred to grill outdoors with friends on the weekends. They had saved $100,000 over ten years, had their home almost paid off, and took one really nice vacation every year.

What was the difference between their thinking and that of Bill and Karen or Susan and Gary? Greg and Liz had decided on the lifestyle they wanted early on in their relationship. They had taken the time to sit down, examine what was important to them, and write it down.

Now, you may be thinking, "That's too much like a contract. What if I change my mind in a year or so?" Then change it! It's not set in stone.

Greg and Liz wanted to take at least one really nice vacation every year. They wanted to be able to splurge and buy souvenirs on their vacations. So, for them, it was more important to save money and live in a neighborhood they were comfortable in so they could afford to take nice vacations. It was not important to them to live in a more upscale neighborhood.

However, Bill and Karen had never thought about the lifestyle or neighborhood question. They had fallen in love with the house, not everything else associated with the location.

Greg and Liz had taken a proactive approach to their life at the beginning of their relationship. They had decided how much money they needed to create the lifestyle they wanted.

But Bill and Karen had never done that. I helped them change their mindset to create a lifestyle more conducive to their happiness.

For me, it's about helping my clients. I could have put together two mortgages and made more money, but that's not what was in the best interests of Bill and Karen. It was about helping them to create the lifestyle they could both enjoy. And it was about doing the same thing for Susan and Gary.

Being a mortgage broker is about helping clients create a lifestyle. I help them figure out how to get from where they are right now to what they really want. The mortgage will come about because of the lifestyle they desire. Here are some questions you want to think about prior to putting an offer on a home and getting a mortgage.

What really makes you happy in a home? In a neighborhood? Consider what is truly important to you in life. Reflect on your core beliefs and principles. Do you believe neighborhoods with kids are going to be loud and full of bicycles and toys in the street, or do you believe a more established, older neighborhood has only elderly people living there? This self-reflection will help you align your lifestyle choices with your values. Knowing these things isn't just for realtors to sell you a home. It also helps a mortgage broker guide you to the home prices you can afford.

What do you think the neighborhood is going to look like in three to five years? Is it going to be full of teenagers or empty nesters? Do you still want to be there in three to five years?

Take stock of your current habits, routines, and choices. Will you be able to exercise, walk, or bike in the neighborhood, or will you need to go to a gym?

If you live in a condo, townhouse, or residential neighborhood with HOA fees, are you going to be able to afford them several years down the road?

Will you or your partner need to have a side hustle or part-time job to afford to live in a specific neighborhood?

Do you like the looks of the neighborhood? How does it make you feel when you drive in it? If you're not wild about driving down the street prior to purchasing a home there, think about how you're going to feel after you've bought it.

As I pointed out earlier, you should take a proactive or offensive strategy to decide what you want in a lifestyle and a home. I want everyone to get what they want, but you have to be willing to work for it. You have to have the mindset of "I'm willing to live in a home like this so I can live like that."

At the same time, I don't think you have to cut, cut, cut and reduce your lifestyle. It's not about clipping coupons or creating a poverty mentality. It's more like realizing that if this is what you want, then let's go get it.

If you need a part-time job or side hustle, then go find a way to make more money. If it's important to you to pay off your home early and not have debt hanging over your head, a mortgage broker can definitely show you ways to do that. By providing access to various mortgage products and assisting with financial planning, mortgage brokers can help you make lifestyle choices that align with your homeownership goals and financial circumstances.

Lifestyle choices are not set in stone. They can evolve as you grow and change. Periodically evaluate your choices and assess their impact on your well-being and fulfillment. It may be time to change neighborhoods. Make adjustments as needed to ensure you're living in alignment with your values.

Remember, determining lifestyle choices is a personal journey, and there is no one-size-fits-all approach. Be patient with yourself, listen to your intuition, and make choices that bring you closer to the life you desire.

Not sure about the type of lifestyle or house you desire? Look for role models or individuals who embody the lifestyle you aspire to have. Engage with communities or groups that share similar interests or values. There are plenty of groups on Facebook or other social media platforms you could join. Look at YouTube videos. Surrounding yourself with supportive and like-minded people can provide encouragement and guidance.

Still greatly desiring a home in a specific neighborhood? I don't blame you; however, you do have to be practical about the numbers. They still have to work for you to obtain a mortgage.

For example, if you and your partner have a gross income of $75,000, you're not going to be able to afford a $400,000 mortgage. You do have to be realistic about the lifestyle and home you want. It still comes down to whether it's more important for you to own a home or to live in a specific neighborhood.

Change your mindset, change your life.

6
TAKING RESPONSIBILITY

UGH! Going from talking about changing your mindset to being able to afford a house to talking about taking responsibility for your actions is not a bad thing. They go together, really.

I'm not going to lie to you: mortgage brokers can't save you from bad choices, and we can't predict the future. Our job is to help you secure a mortgage for the home you want or to help you refinance at a price you can afford.

Judy and Mike came to see me about either refinancing their first mortgage or getting a HELOC (home equity line of credit). They had owned their home for a number of years and were sure they could borrow against the equity in their home. They wanted to use the money to add a deck to the back patio area.

Although I'm a mortgage broker, I'm also considered a loan officer. I own a non-depository company that specializes in residential lending. I have no allegiance to any company or lending institution. I choose what is best for the client based on my relationships with over twenty banks and private moneylenders. These entities are my sources to help you obtain the best mortgage possible.

After reviewing all their financial information, I had the unpleasant task of letting them know that they didn't qualify for the loan. Being a loan officer is not all glitz and glamor. It's great seeing the smiles on the faces of the people who buy homes or are happy with the outcome of refinancing their home, but the other part is the denial.

Mike demanded to know what was involved in my decision to say no to their loan. He thought getting a loan was literally a matter of going to a "mortgage guy" and asking for a specific dollar amount, and he would receive it shortly after that. It doesn't work that way.

To determine whether you can refinance, loan officers must go through the process of reviewing your income, credit history, and equity in your home. We want to help you, but sometimes the outcome is not what you want to hear, though it is the truth. Sometimes during the process, loan officers make discoveries that hinder the possibility of the transaction occurring at the present time. That doesn't mean forever. It just means you must take necessary steps to work toward your end goal. Your goal may be refinancing or becoming a new homeowner.

I never mentioned the possibility that refinancing could help Judy and Mike pay their home off faster because they simply would not qualify at this point. Instead, we spent the next hour going over options to improve their situation.

Mike was not a happy camper, to put it mildly. He was still convinced he should be able to go to the bank and take his equity out. He was probably wondering, *Why did I go to this guy in the first place?* Why didn't I just go to my bank? I explained to both him and Judy why they were not good candidates for a refinance or a HELOC just yet. With access to over twenty-five different banks and lenders, as a mortgage broker with over twenty years of experience, I have many options to assist you in securing the best deal for you. My job is to be honest and help create a plan that we can follow. It is not always what you want to hear, but it does come from a good place.

The key thing to think about is that mortgage brokers are like guidance counselors from school. We are here to guide you along the way. We are not here to do the work. That is still on you. You are the one who must have a good credit score, assets, and a good income. We are merely putting you in the right vehicle to move forward and succeed. You must do the work to put yourself in a good place for a mortgage, and we will help you stay on the path to success. I've heard reasons, aka excuses, throughout my time working with clients for why their situation is the way it is.

"We needed to go on that vacation. I was incredibly stressed at work. The vacation helped me clear my head so I could do better when I got back."

"We needed to take that cruise. Our friends were going, and how could we say no? Plus, we have never been to Cozumel before, and we've always wanted to go on a cruise."

"We had to have the VIP tickets for that concert because she's my favorite performer and who knows if we'll ever get to see her again in concert? After all, this might be the last one she ever does."

Do you see where not taking any type of responsibility for poor spending habits could lead you down the wrong path? Living according to the motto "I see it, I want it, I'll get it" with absolutely no qualms about spending money is a recipe for disaster.

It's not just about taking responsibility for your actions. It's also about knowing what you want: living a specific lifestyle or owning a home. You can certainly do both when you know what's most important to you.

You can do both, and you can do them easily, if you're willing to pay the price and take responsibility for your actions. You must make conscious decisions about what you are going to do, how you are going to spend your money, and what your overall goals are.

You may have to introduce the dreaded word *budget* into your life. Chellie Campbell, author of *The Wealthy*

Spirit, says, "Budget stands for Baby, U Deserve Getting Everything." I agree. When you make financial plans, you can achieve almost anything! This includes the home of your dreams.

You have to be proactive and make a plan to achieve your homeownership goals. Use the SMART method of goal setting. SMART is an acronym for the following traits of good goals.

- SPECIFIC. Vague goals lead to vague results. You have to be very specific in your desires.

- MEASURABLE. Can you measure how close you are to your financial goal? If not, your goal is not specific enough.

- ATTAINABLE OR ACHIEVABLE. Do you believe you can actually achieve your goals? Honestly, if you don't believe your goals are attainable for you (not someone else), then you are right. It won't make any difference how hard you try to make something happen—it won't happen because you don't believe it's possible for you. If you want to change this mindset, start setting small, achievable goals and then acknowledge them to yourself when you do reach them.

- RELEVANT. Do you really want to own your own home? Surprisingly, owning a home is not a big consideration for many people. They are happy living in an apartment or renting a condo or house. A goal has to be important to you, not to anyone else.

- TIME-BASED. When will you achieve your goal? Again, you need to be specific.

For example, Mary wanted to purchase a home, but she didn't know what price range she could afford or what type of neighborhood she wanted to live in, nor was she aware of her time frame to execute the purchase. She was too vague about what she wanted.

As her mortgage broker, I went over the SMART goal method with her. Mary came back with the following specifics: she wanted a townhome in a particular area, she could afford x amount of dollars per month, she had 5 percent of the purchase price she could use as a down payment, and she wanted to move in within sixty days. I helped her to achieve her dream with an Epic mortgage.

When the vision is clear, the results will appear.

7
WHAT'S THE RATE?

"WHAT'S THE INTEREST RATE?" rings in my ears as every client asks that magic question. Everyone wants to know about the interest rates on mortgages. What if I told you that although it's important, it's not the most important thing about a mortgage? The most important thing is whether you can afford the mortgage payment.

Yes, it's true. While mortgage rates matter, it's more essential that you can afford the monthly mortgage payment. For most people, the mortgage payment also consists of other items, such as real estate taxes, homeowner's insurance, and PMI. These items can increase your payment to a point where you can't afford it, so it's not just the interest rate that will impact your monthly payment.

Rates fluctuate every day based on the stock and bond market. The market takes a futuristic look at what may happen. It's too unpredictable to rely on, so the focus should be on your payment. Can you make a mortgage payment? Does the new payment fit into your budget?

Shoshana and Terrelle were looking to purchase their first home together. They had been looking for several months, and the primary holdup was Shoshana. She was a mortgage rate shopper and was adamant that the interest rate was the most important thing in a mortgage loan. Her reasoning was that they would be paying more in interest over the years if the rate was too high. Mortgage rates can always be restructured through a refinance. When you buy a home, you are truly marrying the house and dating the rate.

Terrelle, on the other hand, couldn't care less about the interest rate and was more concerned whether they could afford the monthly payment.

In one sense, they were both correct; however, as I mentioned above, the mortgage rates can always be restructured. I advise my clients to touch base with me every six months and review their current situation to see how things could impact them based on new products or programs that may be available to them.

One thing to consider is your budget at this point. Shoshana and Terrelle needed to review their overall monthly budget and play the what-if game. What if our payments were this? What would change in our lives? What can we cut or do less of to make this work? I see too many people sitting on the sidelines instead of moving forward to a home that would benefit their families in the hopes of getting a lower rate. Control what you can control—the rate is not one of those things.

Again, everything goes back to whether you can afford the monthly mortgage payments. Shoshana only saw the interest rates; Terrelle was looking only at mortgage payment affordability. It's not about who's right or wrong when couples or partners bicker over their point of view. It's about what is right in front of you.

What they both ended up agreeing on was purchasing the house in front of them and making it their home. Success!

8
Mortgage Strategies

MORTGAGES ARE NOT ONE-SIZE-FITS-ALL. As a mortgage broker, once again, I shop around to find solutions to handle your unique financial situation. Your mortgage is unique because it is made to fit you. Mortgage brokers continue to look around for products and programs regularly to expand the portfolio so no family is left behind. We want to help you accomplish your dreams and goals. We set up the plan and work with you so we can make it happen for you!

First-Time Homeowners

Here is a tip for many first-time homeowners: expand your mind to think about other types of properties. Most people think, "I need a single-family residence," but there are just so many more options!

Explore a new option. You could purchase a multi-unit family home. It is still considered a primary residence if you live in one of the units. You may be able to make a down payment as low as 3.5 percent on this type of property. A multi-family residence now becomes a real estate investment for you as you live there, and you obtain cash flow from the other units.

Shemeka is a very successful small business owner with an entrepreneurial mindset. She was in the market for a home and had heard about owning a multi-family home but was unfamiliar with the details when she came to me.

Let me explain what a multi-family home is. It's one building that contains multiple separate "homes." It can range from a duplex (two living units) up to a quadplex (four units). Typically, the owner lives in one unit and rents out the others.

There are many key advantages to owning a multi-family home. The first and most obvious advantage is the rental income. You can rent out the additional units, which can offset your mortgage payments, cover the expenses, and generate a steady stream of income. Generally, in a three-to-four-unit building, you are living rent-free while developing equity in your property.

With multiple units in a multi-family home, if one tenant moves out or fails to pay the rent, you still have other tenants making monthly rent payments to you, and you will be able to make the mortgage payments.

What is really nice about owning a multi-family house is that you can set yourself up as a homeowner and a real estate investor at the same time. Owning this type of property allows you to build equity in what is essentially an investment property. You will potentially benefit from property appreciation over time. As your property value increases, your net worth can grow, and this provides you with an asset that you can leverage in the future.

For example, Shemeka was looking for a long-term strategy for building wealth. Her financial goal was to retire by age fifty-five and travel. She viewed her first acquisition of a multi-family house as a method to achieve her goal. She was beyond ecstatic when she discovered she needed to put down only a 3.5 percent deposit for a multi-family residence. For a straight real estate investment property, lending institutions normally require a 20 to 25 percent down payment.

Check with your certified public accountant for specific advice on your particular financial situation. In general, real estate ownership offers several tax advantages. Specifically, you will be able to deduct mortgage interest, property taxes, insurance, and maintenance expenses. You may also be able to use depreciation on your taxable rental income. Again, check with your accounting professional for your specific financial circumstances.

At some point, you may decide to convert the entire property into a rental investment if your circumstances change and you decide to move into another property.

DOWN PAYMENT ASSISTANCE STRATEGY

I saw my friend Tim from high school for the first time in years. We made small talk and chitchat about family and work. He informed me that he would love to buy a house, but it was just so hard for him to save since he was the only one who worked in his family. He had three kids and a stay-at-home wife. I get it, the struggle to own your own home. I hear that story a lot, but we have a program that can help! Down payment assistance programs are designed to help individuals or families make their down-payment on a house.

The down payment on a house is taken care of via a second mortgage. In some cases, depending on other factors, you may not have to pay back the second mortgage. This cuts the amount you need to bring to closing virtually in half. It's a strategy we can use to reduce the money you need at your closing, and it allows you to still embark on buying a home instead of sitting on the sidelines, waiting. These programs are usually specific to first-time homebuyers, but we have a couple of options to assist others who may need that assistance too.

Some employers offer payment assistance programs as part of their employee benefits package. These programs may include special financing for employee homes. A handful of government assistance programs offer financial aid or grants to help you purchase a home. There may be charities or organizations in your local area that help individuals and families with down payments to own their own homes. It's important to research and explore the available payment assistance strategies specific to your location, needs, and circumstances.

As a mortgage broker, I know of many different programs as well as their eligibility requirements and application processes. In many cases, though, it would take you months to find out about the different programs on your own. Always be up-front and honest with your mortgage broker regarding your financial situation. We can often help you in ways you may not be familiar with.

LEASE OPTION TO PURCHASE

A lease option to purchase is also known as a rent-to-own or lease-purchase agreement. You agree to purchase a home from the landlord while you are renting it. You promise to purchase it at a later date.

In a typical lease option, the landlord and tenant enter into a lease agreement that specifies the terms of the rental period, including the monthly rent amount, the lease duration, and any other conditions.

Often the tenant, the renter, pays the landlord an up-front fee called an option consideration or option money. This fee is typically nonrefundable and is similar to the requirement in an apartment lease agreement to pay the first and last month's rent plus a security deposit at signing. The lease option agreement gives you the opportunity to purchase the property you're renting at an agreed-on purchase price.

The lease period is typically longer than a standard rental agreement and may be from one to three years. During this time, the tenant pays rent as agreed upon in the lease agreement. Part of the rent may be applied as a down payment on the purchase of the property, or it may be a straight rental. It depends on what the landlord and tenant agree to.

You may also have the exclusive right to purchase the property at the agreed upon price before your rental lease ends. Typically, you will have to notify the landlord in writing of your intention to buy.

On a lease option agreement, both the landlord and the tenant sign a purchase agreement outlining the terms of the sale, including the purchase price, financing arrangements, and closing date. Once you and the landlord have agreed on all the details of the transaction, there will be a closing similar to what occurs in a traditional home purchase. You become the homeowner, and the property is transferred to your name. Some common closing costs typically associated with a real estate transaction may also apply to a lease option to purchase arrangement.

One difference between a typical single-family home closing and a lease option to purchase is an option fee. As mentioned above, the buyer typically pays an up-front option fee to secure the right to purchase the property at a later date. This fee is separate from the eventual purchase price and is often nonrefundable. You need to be sure up front and at the time of your agreement whether the option fee will be applied toward the purchase price if you decide to purchase the home. You may also be required to provide a down payment at the time of the eventual purchase. This is typically a percentage of the purchase price and is paid in addition to the option fee.

Please note, you should consult a real estate attorney prior to signing a lease option to purchase. The specific terms and conditions can vary greatly depending on the agreement between the landlord and tenant.

PARTNERSHIPS

Are we in a buyer's market or a seller's market? Real estate changes on a year-to-year basis because of various factors. For example, a new president may take the country in one direction versus the other. In a seller's market, with high demand for properties but low inventory, we see prices of these properties increase. Sometimes, due to the increase in price, a single person will not be able to afford a house on their own.

As I write this book, we are in a seller's market as well as a higher-rate market environment than we have seen for over a decade. This has posed a challenge to many Americans trying to buy homes on their own. Income for most doesn't keep up with the appreciation of the real estate market, so partnerships may be a strategy to consider if you plan on owning or investing in real estate.

Gone are the days of having to be married to secure a mortgage loan. If you and your partner meet the financial requirements of a mortgage loan, you will be approved. It's all about your financial creditworthiness, your credit history, your income level, and the local real estate market conditions.

Anthony and Pat are friends from their days playing football in college. They stayed connected with each other and were both interested in buying a home. However, they were not having any luck on their own finding what they were looking for since they both kept getting outbid and really felt dejected. They had moved into an apartment together so they could reduce the rent costs while they were both still looking individually.

I was on the phone with Anthony and asked him, "While you're looking, is there anyone else that I can help? A friend, family member, or neighbor?"

He told me that Pat, his roommate, was looking. I was kind of surprised that they were both looking at the same time, and this was my first time hearing about this. Good thing I asked. I spoke to Anthony and introduced the concept of a multi-unit property where maybe Anthony could live on the first floor and Pat on the second. He had never considered that option, but combining income increases purchasing power and allows a buyer to qualify for a mortgage more easily. This opened up their entire search.

Two weeks later, Anthony and Pat were back in my office, ready to move forward. They are now happy that they were able to secure a two-unit building and fire their landlord.

GROUP MORTGAGES

Yes, you can obtain a residential mortgage with a group of friends. A joint mortgage, also known as a co-mortgage or group mortgage, is a loan taken out by two or more borrowers for the purchase of residential real estate.

The requirements for this type of mortgage depend on the lender's policies and the specific loan program. Most groups form limited liability corporations (LLCs) when buying together. This is a useful tool when buying investment properties.

The lender assesses each borrower's credit history and credit score. They typically consider the credit profiles of all the borrowers and may be required to use the lowest of all middle credit scores for each applicant when considering interest rates and eligibility.

The lending institution analyzes the debt-service coverage ratio (DSCR) of the property. In layman's terms, the lender wants to know, "Does the cash flow of the property cover the mortgage payment?" If the answer is yes, then more than likely you have yourself a deal. As in a typical residential mortgage, lenders require a down payment for the purchase of the home, typically a multi-family unit.

Sherri, Diana, and Brenda came to me because they had found a small, modest, four-unit multi-family apartment they wanted to purchase. All three of them were single, secretaries in the same office, and in their late twenties. Each had their own apartment and good credit, and they were looking to start their own real estate investment company. This four-unit apartment complex would be their first purchase.

I was able to get them into a mortgage with affordable monthly payments. To say these ladies were ecstatic about their first deal was an understatement! Within nine months, they were looking for a mortgage on another small unit.

To date, they own three small apartment complexes and are still working as secretaries in the same company. They have not changed their lifestyle, nor do they share what they're doing with their co-workers. They are continuing to build their wealth and achieve their dreams one step at a time.

BUY NOW

When I first met with Shoshana and Terrelle in chapter 7, Shoshana was more concerned about the interest rates than the affordability of the mortgage payment. Terrelle and I were finally able to convince her to purchase the house they wanted now. With the housing market so tight in our area, prices were escalating rapidly and there was a strong possibility they wouldn't get the home they wanted at the price they could afford.

My recommendation is always to purchase the home you can afford now. You can always refinance it in years to come. You can restructure the debt with lower payments at a later time.

There are several other reasons why purchasing a home now might be a good decision. Interest rates could always rise, and you might not be able to afford the monthly mortgage payment if that occurs. Also, over time, real estate has proven to be a solid long-term investment. Purchasing now increases the equity in your home as property values appreciate over time.

There are also tax benefits to owning a home. Property taxes and mortgage interest payments are typically deductible on your federal income tax return. Check with your accounting professional for additional advice.

If you are renting, your rent costs will typically increase over time. However, if you buy, your fixed-rate mortgage payments will stay consistent through the term of your loan. You won't have to worry about an increase. This helps you to plan your budget more easily and effectively.

You won't have to worry about moving every year or every couple of years when the rent goes up on an apartment. Again, your fixed-rate mortgage payments will stay consistent throughout the term of your loan.

REVERSE MORTGAGES

A reverse mortgage may be a good strategy for seasoned homeowners. It is designed for those who are at least sixty-two years old and have substantial equity in their homes. The advantage of a reverse mortgage is that it allows homeowners to convert a portion of their home equity into tax-free funds without having to sell their home or make monthly mortgage payments.

Counseling on a reverse mortgage is an independent session conducted by a third party. The counseling aims to ensure that all borrowers and spouses understand what a reverse mortgage is and their obligations when they have one. This helps prevent fraud against the elderly.

While a reverse mortgage can provide benefits to seniors, it's crucial to be aware of the disadvantages. The way a reverse mortgage loan is structured, the loan balance typically increases over time as interest accrues and fees are added to the loan. This means your home equity may decrease over time and leave less equity in the home when the loan is eventually repaid.

As a homeowner, you are still responsible for maintaining the property, paying property taxes, and keeping a homeowner's insurance policy. Ignoring or failing to meet these obligations may lead to a default on your loan and risk foreclosure.

A reverse mortgage can provide many benefits to seniors. It is very complex, and if you are seriously considering obtaining one, you should consult me, a financial advisor, and your family before making a decision.

TEMPORARY 2/1 BUYDOWN

Another strategy to consider is a 2/1 buydown, in which you negotiate a seller concession on a transaction. The seller concession can be used to buy down the interest rate, a whole 2 percent down the first year and 1 percent down the second year. This will give you an adjustment period as a buyer to move into your property and get acclimated to your new budget. You now have a mortgage payment and new utility bills, so it allows you to take advantage of a lower payment for the first two years of homeownership. It's a great way to take advantage of a lower rate initially and gives you another opportunity to see if the interest rate in the market falls below what you currently have. It also allows you to lock into a lower fixed rate by refinancing.

RENOVATION LOANS

Let's say you see a neighborhood that you would love to live in, but the prices are just too high for your budget. Searching for the ugly duckling home that needs tender loving care might be a way for you to get into that neighborhood. If you are willing to spruce up the home with a renovation loan, this is another way to take advantage of all the products that you might have access to by working with a mortgage broker like me.

We do a lot of renovation loans on a yearly basis, and they create instant equity based on the work you're doing. Most dilapidated homes are on the market at a discount. The total purchase price is based on the original purchase price that the seller agreed to sell the property and the renovation costs. The renovation must be done by a licensed and insured contractor. If Uncle Jimmy is not licensed, he's not the one you can call on to do this project. The lender will base everything on the future value of the property, or as some call it, the after-repair value.

The borrower is responsible for getting an appraisal to establish the loan amount and eligibility. You will also have to pay the standard closing agent fees, title insurance fee, recording fees, and consultant fees. A consultant may be appointed to serve as the eyes and ears for the lender. Most lenders lend nationwide, so they need boots on the ground to manage these projects and make sure all is going well.

The beauty of all these strategies is that I have access to assist on all these platforms. With my experience and knowledge of the programs, we can review them along with your financial information and see what would be suitable for your situation.

9
You Have Questions, I Have Answers

ALTHOUGH I ANSWERED many of the common questions below earlier in the book, this chapter gives you a quick reference guide.

1. **MY CREDIT SCORE IS 560, AND I DESPERATELY WANT TO BUY A HOME. IS IT POSSIBLE?**
   Yes, it absolutely is possible! If you need down payment assistance, then the process may take some time, but if you have the necessary funds, then we can proceed. A higher interest rate and large down payment may be in the cards for you; however, if you make your payments on time, your mortgage can be restructured within six months to one year, and your rates may come down. Obviously, the higher the score, the fewer hurdles you may have to jump through, but it can be done.

2. **MY PARTNER AND I HAVE BEEN TOGETHER FOR THREE YEARS, AND WE WANT TO PURCHASE A CONDO. IS THIS POSSIBLE?**

   Yes! If both of you have the necessary credit and have a two-year work history and assets, I should be able to get you a mortgage.

3. **A GROUP OF US GUYS WANT TO BUY AN APARTMENT COMPLEX. CAN WE DO IT?**

   Yes! This is called a group or joint mortgage. If you are looking to purchase it as a multi-family home with five to six units, you will want to create an LLC, and assuming everyone's credit is good, you will be well on your way to your first investment property.

4. **MAY I CALL YOU AND ASK YOU QUESTIONS ABOUT MORTGAGES?**

   Of course! My phone number is (708) 905-5300. I am licensed in Illinois, Indiana, Florida, Colorado, Maryland, Georgia, Michigan, Virginia, and Texas. If you're in another state, I may be working on getting licensed there. Feel free to ask me.

5. **MY GRANDPARENTS WANT TO GIVE ME $25,000 TO USE AS A DOWN PAYMENT ON A HOUSE. DO I HAVE TO PAY TAXES ON THAT?**

    I am not a CPA, so be sure to check with yours. However, based on the rules and regulations of 2023, the IRS has an $11.7 million lifetime exemption for a single person and a $23.4 million combined exemption for married couples before anyone would owe federal tax on a gift or inheritance. In other words, you could give your child $10 million today, and no one would owe any federal gift tax on that amount. Your lending institution may require proof that the money is a gift and not a loan.

6. **WHAT KINDS OF EXPENSES WILL I HAVE AT CLOSING?**

    Typically, you will need to pay the following:
    - Loan origination fee
    - Appraisal fee
    - Credit report fee
    - Mortgage insurance premium
    - Title search
    - Title insurance premium
    - Title examination or abstract fees
    - Lender's title insurance premium
    - Owner's title insurance premium
    - Recording fees

- Transfer taxes
- Property taxes
- HOA fees, if applicable
- Home inspection report cost
- Attorney fees
- Escrow fees
- Other fees, depending on your purchase

7. **WHO CAN HELP ME FINANCE THE PURCHASE OF A HOME?**

There are many different sources. My competitors include banks, credit unions, mortgage lending companies, parents/grandparents, and private lenders. As a mortgage broker, I have access to over twenty-five different banks and lenders to choose from, and this allows you more options in less time. I can help you find the program for your specific situation. So, if you need financing or if someone turned you down, please feel free to reach out.

8. **CAN YOU HELP ME WITH A FINANCIAL PLAN TO GET OUT OF DEBT SO I CAN PURCHASE A HOME?**

Although I am not a certified financial planner, I did work in that industry for over eight years, so I can help you create a budget for paying off credit card debt, establish a savings plan, and find the best mortgage loan program to fit your goals and dreams.

9. **Which is better for a first-time homeowner, a single-family residence or a multi-family unit?**

   It depends on your ultimate goal. There are no right or wrong answers when it comes to the direction you would like to travel when starting your real estate portfolio. Everyone's goals, dreams, and desires are different. Call me at (708) 905-5300 or email me at dante@epic.mortgage, and I'll be happy to help you make the best decision possible.

10. **Are you available for speaking engagements?**

    Absolutely! I love sharing my knowledge of the mortgage industry with others and helping people achieve their dream of owning their own home.

10
THIS IS THE
BEGINNING FOR YOU

WHILE THIS IS THE END OF THE BOOK, it is truly the beginning for you. Knowing a lot more about mortgages, interest rates, credit scores, the loan application process, and how to get ahead financially to achieve your dream of owning a home or a multi-family unit puts you so far ahead of others.

You know what a mortgage broker can do for you and why it's important to have one. You know what to look for to find the right mortgage broker for you.

You now know ways to improve your credit score, mistakes to avoid, and strategies for managing mortgage debt effectively.

You now have answers to the most asked mortgage questions. You also have resources following this chapter. Most importantly, you have me! I can help you through the entire mortgage loan process. All you have to do is ask. Remember, I'm licensed in nine different states and working on becoming licensed in others.

And, lastly, I want to thank you from the bottom of my heart for giving me the opportunity to educate, inform, and help you in the biggest financial decision of your life as you seek to achieve your homeownership dream and your personal and financial goals.

The last step for you to take is action. If you're hesitant about the next action step or have additional questions, feel free to reach out to me, Dante Royster, at (708) 905-5300 or email me at dante@epic.mortgage. You can also visit my website, DanteRoyster.com.

Resources

Get a head start on purchasing your home. Listed below are resources to help you on your exciting journey.

Federal law gives you the right to get a free copy of your credit report every twelve months from each of the three nationwide credit bureaus.

- Equifax   equifax.com
- TransUnion   transunion.com
- Experian   experian.com

Check out your credit score for free at these sites:
- Credit Karma   creditkarma.com
- Annual Credit Report   annualcreditreport.com

To get an idea of how much mortgage you can afford, enter your information in the calculator at:

bankrate.com/mortgages/mortgage-calculator.

ABOUT THE AUTHOR

DANTE provides mortgage products that appeal to a wide range of current and prospective home buyers. His goal is to provide you with the best possible solution for your situation.

People describe Dante as success-driven and a born winner. In working with trusted partners in his business ventures and in his community service activities, he is dedicated to helping develop future leaders and creating lifelong business partners who prosper from each other's success. His dedication is validated in every positive interaction, every testimonial, and every referral he receives. He is also very proud to have been named a Five Star Mortgage Professional in *Chicago Magazine* thirteen years in a row as a result of consumer confidence and exemplary customer service!

Dante's licenses include Illinois Residential Mortgage License MB.6761436, Indiana SOS Loan Broker License #1885086, Florida Mortgage Broker License #MBR3319, Colorado Mortgage Registration License, Maryland Mortgage Lender License #24573, Georgia Mortgage Broker License #1885086, Michigan Mortgage Broker License #FL0023191, Virginia Mortgage Loan License #MC-7586, Texas SML-Mortgage Company License, and Epic Mortgage NMLS 1885086.

He was also a registered representative of FINRA, holding his Series 6 and 63 licensing for eight years. Dante resides in the Chicagoland area. He can be reached at (708) 905-5300 or at dante@epic.mortgage.

www.ingramcontent.com/pod-product-compliance
Lightning Source LLC
Chambersburg PA
CBHW021458180326
41458CB00051B/6868/J